HIST SCOTTISH CHURCHES

other books by the same author:

A Church Near You

A Church Near You in Wales

HISTORIC SCOTTISH CHURCHES

The plight of medieval churches in Scotland

written and illustrated by

DENIS DUNSTONE

with a Foreword by

LORD WALLACE of TANKERNESS

UMBRIA PRESS

First published in 2025 by Umbria Press

Umbria Press
2 Umbria Street
London SW15 5DP
www.umbriapress.co.uk

Designed and typeset in Minion
by Louise Millar

Printed in Poland by Totem
www.totem.com.pl

ISBN 978-1-910074-48-0

Contents

Foreword by **Lord Wallace of Tankerness**

Denis Dunstone's sub-title for his beautifully illustrated book "Historic Scottish Churches" is *"The plight of medieval churches in Scotland."* Initially, it might be thought that this is a contemporary reflection on the dilemma facing churches and congregations the length and breadth of the land, as they try to meet the challenges of maintaining old buildings whilst attendance at worship falls.

Admittedly, there is an echo of today's challenges, but as Mr Dunstone observes in his introduction, *"Even before the Reformation, church buildings in Scotland appear to have been vulnerable to dispute and war, mainly with England."* That history, and the impact of a 'more intense' Reformation in Scotland, leads the author to reflect ruefully, *"Compared with England and Wales, Scotland has fewer Medieval churches surviving."* The figures he cites are stark – England – about 8,000; Wales – nearly 1,000; Scotland – "barely 80".

In an important respect, that makes this book more relevant in providing historic and architectural insights and understanding of this significant part of our Scottish heritage. Whereas in England and Wales, many communities will be familiar with having a medieval place of worship in their midst, that is much less so in Scotland.

I count myself blessed in having been able to worship regularly over the last forty years in the twelfth century St Magnus Cathedral in Kirkwall, Orkney. But even with that degree of familiarity, (or maybe because of it), I nevertheless learned some things new about that spiritually uplifting sacred place.

And as I read about earlier 12th century churches, and then progressed through succeeding centuries, up to the Reformation, my knowledge of ecclesiastical architectural terms and their liturgical significance was greatly enhanced. And for many Scots whose school education in Scottish Medieval history stopped in 1314 or possibly in Arbroath Abbey in 1320, the brief narratives which go alongside the illustrations serve not only to provide historic context but can function as a spur to find out more.

At the book's outset, Mr. Dunstone references Melrose Abbey as epitomising the message of the book. This splendid piece of Scottish Medieval church architecture suffered the consequences of Border warfare and was then left to fall into further post-Reformation ruin; but is now preserved and cared for. Historic Environment Scotland bears the responsibility for maintaining some parts of our church heritage; but there are a number of the medieval churches in this book which are still active places of worship.

Reflecting on their past and the damage done as a consequence of schism, we should recall that their heritage is both Roman Catholic and Presbyterian (and in some cases Episcopalian). Is it too much to hope for that their future might lie in cherishing their respective traditions and becoming beacons of ecumenical reconciliation, united in missionary outreach to the communities they serve?

NATIONAL CHURCHES TRUST

The National Churches Trust helps to keep the UK's chapels and meeting houses open and in use.

Churches are impressive, exciting and surprising places. Whether seeking quiet reflection, access to critical community services, a warm welcome, a place to worship, or a space to explore, we believe they should be loved and supported. Available to all. Working together with churches of all denominations across all four nations, we help to maintain these wonderful historic buildings and keep them thriving today, and tomorrow.

Our charity has a fascinating history that begins at the start of the 19th century with the Incorporated Church Building Society, founded in 1818 to enlarge and build new churches. In 1953 the Historic Churches Preservation Trust assumed responsibility for the society's affairs with a new focus on helping parish churches in a poor state of repair.

The National Churches Trust was created in 2007 to carry on the work of the Historic Churches Preservation Trust (HCPT), which was set up in 1953. Since then we have helped over 2,000 churches with funding for urgent repairs. Our mission is to support and celebrate churches, provide advice and information, and to speak up for churches of all Christian denominations and the work they do. Our supporters include Sir Michael Palin, Hugh Dennis and Bill Bryson. We were honoured that HM Queen Elizabeth was our Patron throughout her reign.

If you love churches, you can support our work and help more churches stay open by becoming a Friend. Find out more at nationalchurchestrust.org

SCOTLAND'S CHURCHES TRUST

Scotland has a very different religious history from other parts of the UK and this is reflected in our sacred buildings and their contents. This new guide introduces readers to some of Scotland's surviving medieval churches, where history, architecture, community and faith intertwine to tell the story of our nation's rich cultural and built heritage. It is an important addition, providing a useful and well-illustrated listing.

In the late 1970s broadcaster and author Magnus Magnusson, and others, founded the Scottish Architectural Heritage Trust (SCAHT) as this distinctive building tradition was endangered and lacked the support network that existed for churches south of the Border. Just over a decade later, this heritage charity was joined by the Scotland's Churches Scheme (SCS). SCAHT primarily concentrated on providing maintenance grants and advice for churches with SCS focussed on supporting appreciation of the heritage and growing Scotland's religious tourism.

The two charities merged in 2012 to form Scotland's Churches Trust, with HRH The Princess Royal as our patron. Since the earliest days of both bodies, we have grown, nurtured and supported a nationwide network of places of worship, of all denominations, widening the public's appreciation of church heritage in Scotland.

From the medieval to the modern, we continue preserving, promoting and protecting Scotland's unique religious built heritage, endeavouring to ensure that all of these precious and treasured sacred buildings remain in use and at the heart of their communities for generations to come.

If you would like to find out more about us or support our work, please visit our website (www.scotlandschurchestrust.org.uk) or follow us on one of our social media channels.

Founded in the 12th century and tormented by a succession of English kings, Melrose Abbey is a symbol of how the splendours of Scottish Medieval architecture have suffered. The preserved ruins of the 14th century building are magnificent in their agony having been left to die after the Reformation. They are now preserved and cared for and epitomise the message of this little book, which seeks to cast sympathetic light upon what remains of Scottish Medieval church architecture.

Typical church layout

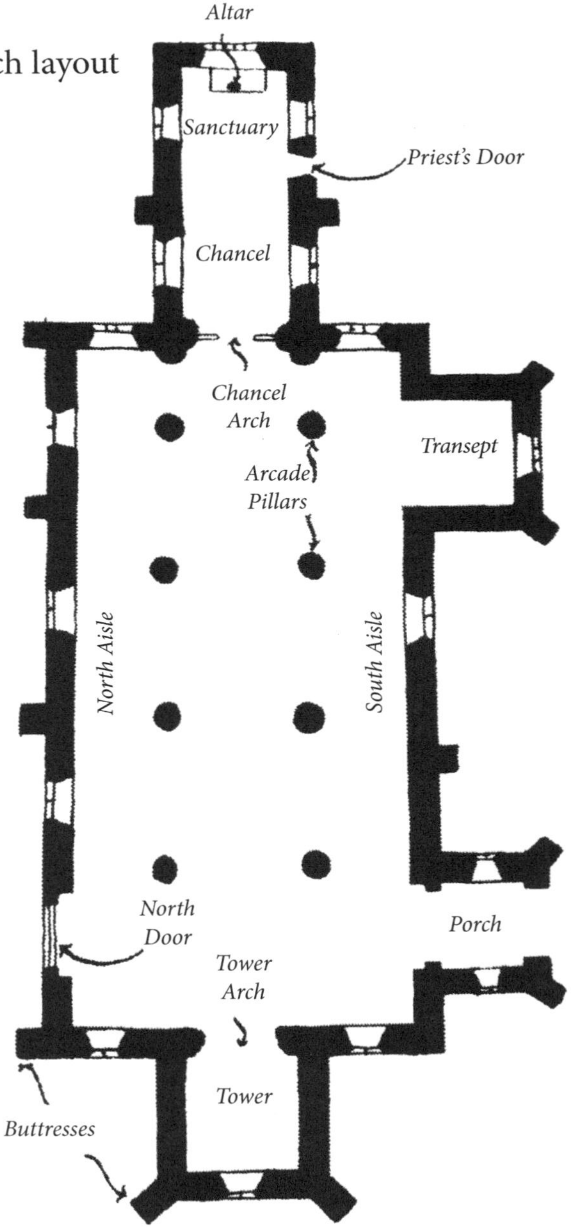

Introduction

Previous books in this series covered Medieval churches in England and Wales and sought to introduce them in lay-man's terms to an audience who may have been quite unaware of the characteristics of buildings with which they were superficially quite familiar. This book picks up the thread and covers surviving Medieval churches in Scotland in similar terms.

This book concentrates on the exterior of churches as that is where building history is best revealed.

With some notable exceptions it eschews ruins, though there are many. Here the approach is by age, rather than by features such as layout, towers and doorways. This is partly due to the smaller total number and partly because of the interest to be found in the comparison with what went on across the border.

The biggest difference is the amount of damage done to Scottish churches, often by the English, but there was also a completely different attitude to church buildings brought about by the nature of the Reformation in Scotland.

Christianity reached Scotland in the 5th century. As it came from Ireland, the earliest churches were on the west coast and in the islands. Christians from Europe arrived in England in the 6th century in the wake of St Augustine, but by the 7th century the differences between these two sources had been reconciled at a Synod in Whitby.

As Christianity spread, Scottish local churches tended to remain much simpler than their English counterparts, though all were initially made of wood. There was a preference for the simple square-ended nave and chancel, called in England Celtic.

By the 8th century masonry was being used. From the 12th century, there were a few larger Romanesque buildings, such as Dunfermline Abbey and St Magnus Cathedral in Orkney. But apart from one case in St Andrews the Anglo Saxon style did not penetrate Scotland. Norman on the other hand was widely seen.

From the 13th century the European Gothic style with pointed arches and windows began to appear in Scotland. Later Gothic produced a massive style often cruciform and with an apse, that may have been influenced by contacts with the continent. It was quite different from the contemporary English Perpendicular style and there were no tall spires.

This book like its predecessor on English churches is confined to the period leading up to the Reformation in the 16th century. Even before the Reformation, church buildings in Scotland appears to have been vulnerable to dispute and war, mainly with England. A smaller proportion of these have survived intact because the Reformation in Scotland was more intense and led eventually to a complete abandonment of Catholicism in favour of a more communal and less ritualistic style of worship. In England the Protestant successor was expressly Catholic, though independent from Rome. Consequently although the monasteries suffered, its churches remained largely intact. Non-conformism grew independently and not as part of the national church.

The consequence is that compared with England and Wales, Scotland has far fewer Medieval churches surviving. In England there are about 8,000, of which most have received alterations over time, especially in the 19th century. In Wales there are nearly 1,000, the majority of which have been rebuilt in the 19th century. In Scotland there are barely 50.

Chapter 1:
Beginnings and Twelfth Century

The earliest surviving church buildings in Scotland are from the 12th century. Many of the more remote small churches of this period have become ruined or nothing but footings. Those in more densely inhabited areas were altered or demolished to make room for a replacement.

During the 12th century smaller buildings were simply rectangular in format, with and without a separate choir at the east end. There were also reflections of Irish origins in towers. Windows and doorways were Romanesque in style as in England and in larger churches the Gothic style began towards the end of the century. But in general, as in England, transition was slow and this was predominantly the Norman period.

The oldest church in Edinburgh is St Margaret Chapel in Edinburgh Castle. It is built of stone and has round-topped Norman windows as found in England already in the 11th century.

It was built in the 12th century and has an unusual feature in the form of an internal apse. The semi circular apse was a Continental feature introduced to Britain after St Augustine. It became popular in Scotland much later, especially when polygonal.

Among the earliest survivors from the 12th century, is the Anglo Saxon style St Rule in St Andrews.

This bears many of the characteristics found in English church towers of the 11th century: a tall narrow shape, long and short work on the quoins (comers), that is stones laid alternatively either way. In this case this feature is less obvious because all the stones are neatly cut. The double belfry opening differs slightly from the English examples by having supporting masonry between the arches rather than a stone column.

The Anglo Saxon belfry opening has variants in Scotland as seen at St Droston, Markinch in Fife and St Serf's Dunning, south of Perth. Markinch also has an early stone spire.

St Droston, Markinch

St Serf's, Church, Dunning

Late in the 11th century or early in the 12th two towers were built, one at Abernethy south of Perth seen above, and the other at Brechin.

Their role is not certain but it is likely that they served as a belfry for the neighbouring churches and also as a look-out. This was a common practice in Ireland.

A number of 12th century churches survive though usually altered. In order to see the original format it is often necessary to have recourse to ruins. One of the better preserved ruins is on Egilsay in Orkney. Here St Magnus is a Norse foundation with a round tower characteristic of the churches in Ireland. Inspite of the unusual tower, the church has the typical Celtic layout of square ended choir and nave, sometimes with a west tower. This format is now seen in 85% of English churches.

The saddleback tower of Muthill Church, west of Perth, was built in the 12th century. The nave was rebuilt in the 15th century with notably large Gothic arches. It survived the Reformation but in the 19th century it was decided to build a new church. At the same time an Episcopal church was built, both of them making use of the stones of the old church.

The tower is one of the most impressive Norman towers in Scotland and in its height has something of the Anglo Saxon.

A more perfect example of the Celtic style Norman church is St Fillans at Aberdour near Burntisland in Fife, especially when seen from the north. The north transept is later.

An aisle was added on the south side with very low eaves; from that angle they give the church an appearance similar to some in the south of England, especially in Sussex. This effect is emphasised by the fact that the floor of the church is down three steps from ground level. Inside the church is quiet and dark and manages to have an eerie stillness.

The bell cote is typical of small churches unable to afford the cost of building a tower.

Norman churches were in the Romanesque style with roundtopped vaults, arches and windows. This continued into the 13th century.

St Mungo's at Stobo near Peebles is another 12th century church, but in this case there has been considerable alteration since the Reformation. On the south side Gothic windows have replaced the Norman, the saddleback tower has been raised, and on the north side an odd Arts and Crafts north transept has been added.

As an economic means of increasing light, dormer windows have been introduced.

At Uphall in West Lothian a 12th century church remains intact, though transepts have been added. There are distinctly Norman doorways into the tower and on the south side of the nave. The saddleback tower is unusual in having a bell cote on top of it.

St Athernase at Leuchars in Fife has a magnificent Norman apse and chancel from the 12th century, though most of the rest of the church is from the 19th century.
The turret stuck on top of the apse is from the 18th century.

Across Scotland there was a virtually standard pattern of Celtic country churches. Legerwood is near Lauder in the Borders and retains many Norman features.

Birnie in Elgin, Moray was once the seat of a Bishop.

Symington Kirk in Lanark although altered is interesting for its early curved apse. Symington in Ayrshire has its bell cote at the east end. Apart from the later transept, it has original features, especially the windows. Both churches were founded by the same Symon.

St Mary Monymusk is west of Aberdeen with strong Norman credentials in its windows. It was originally attached to an Augustinian Monastery, hence the long chancel which was later shortened. The twin openings in the tower which superficially look as thought they might be Anglo Saxon are in fact an example of the Norman twin openings.

Duddingston near Edinburgh has a similar layout but the Gothic windows are later, as are the buttresses attached to what were originally pilasters (flat columns). The pinnacles are also later. Notable is the surviving Norman south doorway, now blocked up.

Kirkliston in West Lothian has a 12th century church with a tower. It was lowered when the saddleback roof was installed and there are some very unsuitable windows. However it is redeemed by its magnificent Norman south door of quite extraordinary size. It is also unusual in having an external tower access turret and a bell-cote stuck on top of the tower (like Uphall). The transept is not original.

An even finer example is at Dalmeny near Queensferry in Midlothian. Here there is an almost perfect unadulterated church dedicated to St Cuthbert. Only the tower is not original though it is entirely compatible. This church has an original curved apse. Many of these have been destroyed as a number of chancels were extended in the 13th century at the expense of the apse, as happened in Kirkwall. Some curved apses have survived in England, but in Scotland it was the polygonal apse which was to become popular 200 years later.

Inchcolm, a small island in the Firth of Forth, was the site of a monastery founded in the 12th century. The nave of the abbey church is roofless and ruined but the corbelled tower and east gable survive; the monastery itself is remarkably complete, perhaps because it was more difficult to take the stone away from a windswept island.

The two largest Romanesque Norman churches in Scotland are at Kirkwall in Orkney and Dunfermline in Fife. Their fate has been in sharp contrast. St Magnus Kirkwall is a cathedral and almost complete, apart from the loss of its apse when the chancel was extended in the 13th century. Even the style of the original typically Scottish spire was replicated in the 20th century. Orkney and Shetland were ruled by Norway from the 8th century until 1472.

On the other hand, at Dunfermline the wonderful Norman nave, similar to that at Durham Cathedral, stands separated from the new construction at the east end. Supported by massive buttresses it is no longer treated as part of the church and is managed by Historic Scotland. East of the nave, only the walls of the apse survive, though only in part. The east end suffered damage in the Reformation and over time collapsed. It was replaced in the 19th century with a quite different building in English Perpendicular style .

The west towers are later replacements.

This sketch of the east end of Dunfermline Abbey emphasises the remains of the original apse which sits uncomfortably beneath the east window of the 19th century church.

There is a small chapel at the north end of Lewis dedicated to St Moluag, with Norman Romanesque windows and doorway. It is an Episcopalian church which only functions in the summer months as it has no electricity supply.

Chapter 2:
Thirteenth Century

At the end of the previous century England was introduced to the Gothic style, the pointed arch, window and vaults. It came from France, and it was the rebuilding by a Frenchman of the chancel of Canterbury Cathedral at the end of the 12th century which started the trend.

It was gradual and in smaller churches the change was less obvious. In Scotland it was initially mainly the larger buildings which saw the change. There are examples of buildings with both Norman and Gothic features built during the course of the 13th century. Later, Gothic prevailed and pointed windows became universal until the Renaissance in the 17th century. This brought classical forms, Greek columns and round arches. Gothic returned in the 18th and 19th centuries and became a widespread indicator of a building functioning as a place of Christian worship, non-conformist or episcopal.

Jedburgh Abbey is here seen from the north west. Now roofless, it was built during the change of styles and its east end, built first, was Romanesque while the nave was Gothic. The west door was nevertheless a fine example of Romanesque. The clerestory (first row up) windows are a rare combination with round arches each embracing two pointed windows.

The north transept, pure Gothic came later.

The west end of Brechin Cathedral is a fine example of Gothic style. Built in the 13th century, it stands beside the second of the Scottish towers.

The future of this building is uncertain as it has recently been closed for worship.

St Mungo's Cathedral in Glasgow is the oldest building in the city and the oldest cathedral on the mainland. This is remarkable as it is also very large. The site is thought to have had Christian associations since the 6th century.

The present building was founded in 1136 but most of the construction took place in the 13th century and 14th. The wooden spire was struck by lightning in the 15th century, whereupon the stone spire was built, notable for the number of lucemes (small windows let into the spire). It has a superficial resemblance to the cathedral in Kirkwall with central tower, cruciform layout and aisles from end to end. There is an ambulatory at the east end projecting at ground floor level, as seen also at Rosslyn Chapel.

It is in the care of Historic Scotland though used by the Church of Scotland for services. The original twin west towers were demolished in the 19th century leaving Aberdeen as the only functioning example in Scotland, Elgin being by then a ruin and the west end of Dunfermline a museum.

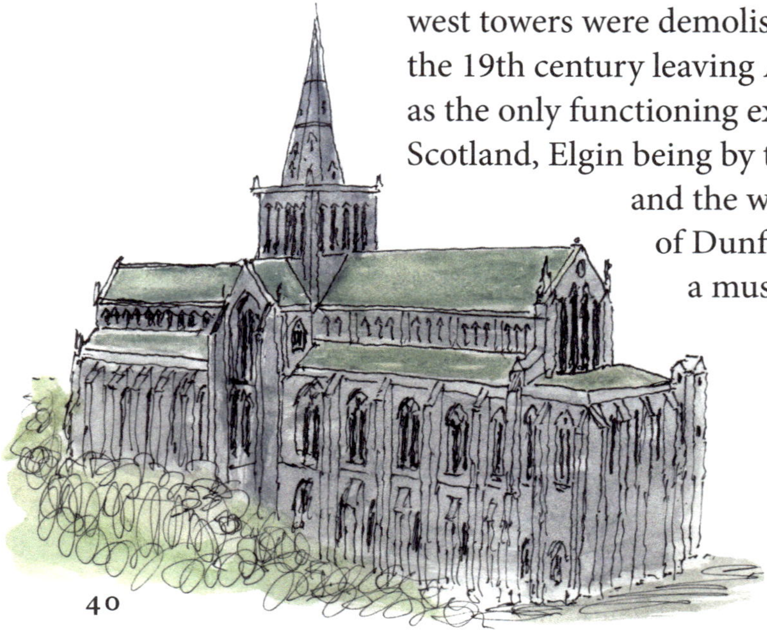

Perhaps the greatest loss since the Reformation is the Cathedral at Elgin. The lead from the roof was the first to go and thereafter deterioration set in. The central tower collapsed in 1711 destroying the nave. It was not until the 20th century that serious restoration began.

This was a cruciform church with central tower and twin west towers, and with spires on all three. The west towers are the earliest part and were built in the early 1200s with early Gothic windows. Later that century Norman windows continued to be built in the south transept contrasting with large Gothic windows on the south side of the nave.

Torphichen Preceptory was founded in the 12th century for the knights Hospitaller of the Order of St John of Jerusalem. It had a cruciform church built in the 13th century. The nave continued to be used as a church after the Reformation until the 18th century. It was then demolished and a new church was built. This can be seen to the left above, with the original tower and transepts behind. The original choir was demolished. There are Gothic windows in the transept.

At Cullen on the coast of Moray the Gothic arrived mid-13th century. The south transept has lancet windows and the east end has a large three light window with tracery.

Culross Abbey in Fife was a Cistercian Monastery built in the 13th century.

Like the cathedrals at Elgin and Glasgow it was cruciform, but without aisles. In about 1500 the nave was demolished as its use was no longer required by the monastery. It was replaced with a tower. The chancel and transepts remain. After the Reformation the east end became the parish church. The monastic ruins are in the care of Historic Scotland.

The lower four levels of the tower of Dunblane Cathedral were built in the 11th century, but the nave and choir were a creation of the 13th, with early Gothic windows. The tower was completed in the 15th century. Originally the tower was free-standing, hence its unusual position. Following the Reformation the nave became disused and the roof fell in. It remained a ruin until it was restored in the 19th century. It is the property of the state, not the Church of Scotland.

Dunblane is just north of Stirling and has eight churches, a large number for a small town of 9000 people.

Crail Church in Fife began in the 12th century as a small Romanesque aisle-less church. In the 13th century it was enlarged with two arcades creating aisles which are a rare feature in Scotland. The tower was built at that time and is of a style popular in Scotland. The corbelled parapet and spire were added in the late 15th or early 16th century.

In the 19th century large pointed windows were installed in the south aisle, while in the north aisle (the side rarely seen by the public) there are simply domestic style square windows. They give good light but undermine the medieval character of the church; a dormer above the south door does even more.

Dunkeld Cathedral is in a large village on the north bank of the Tay, north of Perth. Construction started late 13th century and took over a hundred years. In spite of its late start it has some Romanesque features including the rare blind arcade above the nave arches; this contains within Romanesque arches twin Gothic windows. This is also a feature at Jedburgh where they serve as a clerestory. The tower is from the 14th century and is unusually set against the north aisle.

The nave is now roofless and Church of Scotland services are held in the choir which functions as the parish church.

The building is classified as an Ancient Monument and is a Crown Property administered by Historic Scotland.

The Isle of Iona, off the coast of Mull is where Christianity began in Scotland, when monks arrived there from Ireland in about 560. It has been a centre of Christianity for centuries and has had a turbulent history. The present abbey is the result of a restoration in the 19th century of a 13th century cruciform building which had become semi-ruinous.

The small building with a fine Romanesque doorway is a chapel to St Oran, built in the 12th century.

The Bishop of Ross commanded a vast diocese across Scotland based at Fortrose and built the main part of the cathedral in the 13th century. The south aisle which survives was added in the 14th century.

After the Reformation the lead from the roof was sold off and Cromwell stole much of the masonry; the building gradually deteriorated. We are left with an impressive red sandstone south aisle in the hands of the state with prominent Gothic window spaces.

Another ruined 13th century church is at Inchmahome. This is in a monastery on an island in a lake near Aberfoyle. In this case the Gothic style five light east window is in contrast with the west doorway and arcading. This feature was popular for east windows as seen in Glasgow and Dornoch Cathedrals.

Dornoch Cathedral is seen here from the south east. It is an early example of the cruciform layout. In England the Normans started to build them a century earlier, in some cases by adding transepts to an existing axial church. The nave of Dornoch was destroyed by fire in the 16th century and the whole building was restored in the 19th century. The new nave is narrower than its predecessor.

Pluscarden Priory is near Elgin. Founded in the 13th century as a Benedictine Monastery, it has had a turbulent history. After the Reformation it passed into private ownership, declined and became ruinous; masonry was removed and, having been originally cruciform, it lost its nave.

After 1948 it was restored and given to a holy order. It now functions as an active Benedictine monastery.

The sketch above is from the north west.

Coldingham Priory in south east Scotland was founded in the 11th century and was a large institution. The church was destroyed in 1216 by King John. It was replaced by a larger church which was partially destroyed in 1545, again by the English. Oliver Cromwell finished the job in 1650. Only the north and east walls still stood.

In the 17th century the church was restored.

The surviving arch was the connection between the south transept and the south aisle of the nave.

St Ternan's Church at Arbuthnott in Aberdeenshire is substantially a 13th century church. In 1500 the west tower was added together with the two level south burial transept. This unsympathetically large addition is in the form of an apse

St Vigeans Church near Arbroath was consecrated in 1242. The tower and aisles were added later. In the 19th century the apse was added and alterations were made to the windows.

Chapter 3:
Fourteenth Century

In this century there was a continuation of the upgrading of old foundations and the Gothic style continued. In England the first more simple Gothic style (called Early English) had been overtaken by the more elaborate Decorated style. In Scotland a similar development occurred in larger churches towards the end of the century, though with distinctive styles of tracery. After the Black Death epidemic in 1350, England saw marked economic growth based on wool.

Simultaneously a new style of Gothic emerged with large windows, flatter arches and elaborate fan-vaulting, known as Perpendicular. This was not repeated in Scotland, or indeed anywhere in the world other than north east Wales.

In Scotland this century saw the cruciform layout extended. A fine example which was never completed and remained without a nave stands on the edge of the coast of Fife at St Monans.

Generally there was little church building in this century, perhaps due to problems with the English.

St Monans in a commanding position by the Firth of Forth has a typical Scottish tower with a short spire. By the time of the Reformation the cruciform layout, but without a nave, was perhaps more suited to the new Church of Scotland than a complete cruciform layout.

Its future is uncertain as it was recently put up for sale.

Only the choir survives at St Brides, Douglas in Lanarkshire. This was a collegiate church by which is meant that it was served by a number of priests who were employed to pray continually for the soul of the founder.

The tower was built in the 16th century and has the oldest working clock in Scotland. It is said to have been a donation from Mary Queen of Scots.

At Tain on the south side of the Dornoch Firth, St Duthus Church is elaborately decorated with gabled buttresses and large Gothic windows.

The gabled buttress appears also at Dornoch Cathedral and elsewhere and seems to have been markedly popular in Scotland where they are called gablets.

The abbey church at Fearn, south east of Tain, is in contrast minimal Gothic with lancet windows and a four light east window. The south transept is a ruin.

It is for sale and closed for services.

The first Christian activity in Paisley occurred in the 6th century. It was followed in the 12th century by a priory. Having been burnt down by the English King Edward I, it was replaced with the abbey with a cruciform layout. During the 15th and 16th centuries a number of fires caused the fabric to deteriorate, the tower collapsed and only the western end could be used for services.

In the 19th century the building was restored to its original form. The west door has survived from the 12th century building

In Aberdeen the first Christian site of worship was established by St Machar in 580. Later, a Romanesque church was built in the 12th century. In the 14th century this building was demolished and replaced by a building with twin west towers, a nave, aisles, a north transept and a chancel. A start was made on the central tower. The western spires were built in the 15th century.

Twin west towers were a common feature for cathedrals in England and France, but these and Dunfermline are the only survivors on an active cathedral building in Scotland.

As a result of the Reformation the chancel was demolished and lead from the roof was sold. The central tower collapsed in a storm in 1688 destroying the transepts and chancel. As a result the west end of the nave was closed off. The ruins are in the care of Historic Scotland. The nave remains in use as a church.

Note that there is a parvise over the south porch as at Perth.

In 1825 the tower of St Peter's Inverkeithing in Fife survived a fire which ruined the rest of the church. It was rebuilt in record time by 1827. Here is another Scottish tower with typical spire, but it is a pity about the clocks.

In spite of the low level of church building at this time there was a major new construction at St Giles in Edinburgh. An earlier church was replaced by a large building with aisles and a central tower. The two south aisles and north aisles with chapels occupy the width of the transepts and thus disguise the basic cruciform layout. In the late 15th century the tower was made higher and given the crown steeple modelled on that at Newcastle on Tyne. Further improvements were made in the 19th century including the great west doorway.

John Knox was Minister here when the Scottish Reformation started in 1560. The church then suffered from religious controversy and was used in part for secular activities. In the 19th century it was tidied up and its dignity was restored.

Chapter 4:
Fifteenth Century

This century saw a surge in church building, particularly of larger churches, where replacements of small earlier constructions were built. The cruciform layout as at Paisley and Edinburgh became fashionable. This coincided with the extension of the Perpendicular in England. Perth, Stirling and Haddington are prime examples but there were a number of smaller churches in this style, mostly in East Lothian.

At the same time the polygonal apse became popular. It was not popular in England at this time so the conclusion must be that the near Continent was the source of inspiration. This could also account for the late enthusiasm for the cruciform layout.

At the end of the 15th century and at the beginning of the 16th, Aberdeen University Kings College chapel was built with a crown spire. It had to be replaced in the 17th century, but has became a popular and memorable feature of the university. The chapel lies along the north side of the main quadrangle and has a slightly ungainly appearance.

It is also notable for its apse and the attractive way the buttresses follow the curved shape of the crown.

Aberdeen roof tops lead to St Nicholas Church in the distance. This church was founded in the 12th century but mainly built in the 15th. It was rebuilt in the 18th and 19th centuries, so no medieval work is visible outside. Only the crossing is original.

St John's in Perth is a good example of the cruciform layout with unique styling at the west end. It has north and south aisles. It is also remarkable for having an upper storey on the north porch called in England, where it was quite common, a parvise. The tower, while typically Scottish, has a broach spire, a clever device for reducing six sides to four to fit the tower.

The Church of the Holy Rude, Stirling is another cruciform example. In this case a central tower was intended but was never built; a west tower was built instead. The choir is significantly higher than the nave and the west tower has a prominent turret. There is also a polygonal apse, formidably high due to the fall in the ground.

The collegiate church at Crichton in Midlothian was built cruciform but the nave, if it was ever built, is a ruin. This is a church which is privately owned but can be hired for weddings.

The nave of Trinity Kirk in Edinburgh was never built. This is how the church appeared shortly before it was pulled down to make way for Waverley Station in 1848. Subsequently, after being largely rebuilt elsewhere in the city, it was again pulled down and only one transept and some windows from the apse survive.

Cruciform Dunglass Kirk, near the coast between Edinburgh and Berwick, is almost complete. However, after the Reformation it fell out of use and in the 18th century became a farm building. At this time the east window and its surrounds were demolished.

It is privately owned and functions as a windowless wedding venue. The north side is showing signs of damp.

Fifteen miles distant and nearer to North Berwick, cruciform St Mary's Whitekirk is the result of a major reconstruction of a 12th century church.

At one time a place of pilgrimage, its future is uncertain as the village has a small population. It was refurbished and re-roofed after a serious fire caused by suffragettes in 1914.

There is yet another cruciform church east of Edinburgh at Port Seton. This was a collegiate church built on the remains of an older church but never completed. This is another church without a nave, and the coming of the Reformation prevented the completion of the spire.

There are no windows facing east in the transepts and once again there are signs of damp. It has the then fashionable polygonal apse.

At the time St Mary's was built in Haddington, east of Edinburgh, it was the fourth largest town in Scotland. The church is the longest in the country (206 ft.long.) With aisles the length of both nave and choir it has a massive appearance and its cruciform layout is partially disguised.

St Mary's in Dundee is another cruciform church. It has had a violent history, being burnt down twice. As a result only the tower is from the 15th century, the rest being from the 19th.

Although it is a Church of Scotland church, it has been divided between three separate congregations, now reduced to two, one at the east end, the other at the west. The same happened in Glasgow Cathedral.

Aberlady Kirk on the coast of East Lothian is not a cruciform church though it looks like one. The aisles have the external appearance of transepts. The typically Scottish tower was built in the 15th century with nave and choir, but these were demolished in the 18th century. The replacements lasted until the 19th century, when it was rebuilt.

The belfry opening in the tower is distinctly Saxon in style.

St Clement's in Rodel in Harris was built at the end of the 15th century and at the beginning of the 16th. It has transepts but is not truly cruciform as there is no central crossing. It served as a Catholic church for only a short time before the Reformation when it fell into disuse. In the 19th century it served as a cattle shelter until it was restored by a local aristocratic lady.

It is now in the hands of Historic Scotland.

The Priory Church at South Queensferry was built in connection with a Carmelite Monastery. After the Reformation it was used as the parish church until the 17th century when a new church was built. It fell into disuse and its nave was demolished and the top of the tower removed. It was saved in the 19th century when it was partially restored and became an Episcopal church.

As the chancel is now the nave and the south transept a baptistry, it is unusual in having the congregation face west.

St John's Collegiate Church at Corstorphine near Edinburgh is inadvertently cruciform in layout. The North transept and a north aisle were added in the 19th century. At the same time the rare west porch was built using stone from a 12th century predecessor on the site. The spire is octagonal. The roofs are made of stone.

Tullibardine Chapel between Stirling and Perth was a private chapel of the Murray family. As such it survived the Reformation and is still privately owned though in the care of Historic Scotland.

St Nicholas Dalkeith near Edinburgh was built in the 15th century when it became a parish church. Originally there was a chapel on the site, which became a collegiate church in the 15th century.

St Nicholas is perhaps the most English of Scottish churches. It is certainly full of interest. Its broach spire could have come from Northamptonshire with its height and lucemes (gabled windows). The gabled buttress (gablet) was a feature in both countries.

It is cruciform like its Scottish contemporaries of this time, and the Gothic windows have distinctly Scottish tracery, but it has north and south aisles, more English than Scots.

It has an elaborate south porch, but best of all it has a polygonal apse. After the Reformation this was allowed to deteriorate and it is now roofless. In England it would have been either demolished or completely restored.

St Matthew's Collegiate Chapel in the village of Roslin, Midlothian, is the chancel of a private church intended to be cruciform but never completed. Now known as the Rosslyn Chapel it is the most exotic church in Scotland.

After the Reformation it continued in use by the Sinclair family who were Roman Catholics. In the 17th century Cromwell used it to stable his horses, and later a local Protestant mob caused more damage. It was finally closed at the beginning of the 18th century. Queen Victoria visited it in 1842 and declared it should be restored. Twenty years later it re-opened as an Episcopal church administered by a trust. Some have called it Scotland's answer to the Sainte Chapelle in Paris. It is unique in Britain and now attracts well over 100,000 visitors a year.

A fine porch was built at the west end when it was no longer intended to build the rest of the church.

St Michael's Linlithgow in West Lothian is a large church with aisles and transepts and with a polygonal apse. It also has a parvise over the south porch with an oriel window. It is adjacent to Linlithgow Palace and had considerable contact with royalty before the Reformation. It replaced an earlier building which was destroyed by fire in 1424.

On top of the tower there was originally a crown spire similar to that on St Giles Edinburgh, but in 1821 it was decided that it was unsafe and it was removed. In 1964 a new interpretation was erected. The sketch on the next page shows the tower as it was before 1820 and is based on a painting by Edward Blore.

Ladykirk Church near Coldstream and the River Tweed owes is quality of design and construction to King James IV on whose orders it was built. It is rare in having a stone roof and polygonal transepts, besides a similar-shaped apse, and buttresses topped with pinnacles. The tower is unusual.

Chapter 5:
Sixteenth Century

This was now on the verge of the Reformation. In England the break with the Pope was in 1536. It not until 1560 that John Knox led the Scottish break with Rome. This had a serious effect on church building. In future churches were designed for the more communal style of worship. This often meant a continuation of style, especially for small churches, but until the emergence of the Episcopal church in the 19th century, Scottish churches tended to be functional meeting places and lacked medieval mystery and grandeur.

The ruinous Castle Semple church in Renfrewshire was founded as a collegiate church in 1504. The polygonal apse was added in the 16th century with narrow Gothic windows. These are repeated on the north side of the nave. The roof was taken off in the 19th century due, it is suggested, to the decline in the local population.

Shortly after that a private chapel was built at Innerpeffray near Crieff. After the Reformation it survived as a private Roman Catholic chapel, partly because the first public library in Scotland was installed upstairs, and partly because it was used as a Drummond burial vault. The library is now next door.

Similar simple barn-like churches were built at his time, some of which survive intact.

Mid Calder Church in West Lothian was started in 1541, but only the chancel was completed. In 1863 the belfry and transept were added. The nave was never built. At that time the 'monstrous carbuncle' of a vestry was added on the end of the impressive polygonal apse.

What it might have become can be seen at Biggar in Lanarkshire. It was completed after the English had broken with Rome in 1546 and was the last pre-reformation church built in Scotland. It is cruciform with a central tower, a polygonal apse at the east end, and a south door with a porch.

The tower is castellated, a style popular in England from the 13th century but less common in Scotland. There is also a prominent turret for access to the belfry.

Index *Locations listed by council area*